THE
PRINCIPAL 50

Critical Leadership
Questions *for*
Inspiring Schoolwide
Excellence

THE PRINCIPAL 50

Critical Leadership Questions *for* Inspiring Schoolwide Excellence

BARUTI K. KAFELE

Alexandria, Virginia USA

1703 N. Beauregard St. • Alexandria, VA 223111714 USA
Phone: 800-933-2723 or 703-578-9600 • Fax: 703-575-5400
Website: www.ascd.org • E-mail: member@ascd.org
Author guidelines: www.ascd.org/write

Judy Seltz, *Executive Director,* Stefani Roth, *Publisher;* Genny Ostertag, *Director, Content Acquisitions;* Julie Houtz, *Director, Book Editing & Production;* Ernesto Yermoli, *Editor;* Donald Ely, *Senior Graphic Designer;* Mike Kalyan, *Manager, Production Services;* Keith Demmons, *Desktop Publishing Specialist;* Kelly Marshall, *Production Specialist*

All web links in this book are correct as of the publication date below but may have become inactive or otherwise modified since that time. If you notice a deactivated or changed link, please e-mail books@ascd .org with the words "Link Update" in the subject line. In your message, please specify the web link, the book title, and the page number on which the link appears.

PAPERBACK ISBN: 978-1-4166-2014-3 ASCD product #115050   n3/15

PDF E-BOOK ISBN: 978-1-4166-2016-7; see Books in Print for other formats.

Quantity discounts: 10–49, 10%; 50+, 15%; 1,000+, special discounts (e-mail programteam@ascd.org or call 800-933-2723, ext. 5773, or 703-575-5773). For desk copies, go to www.ascd.org/deskcopy.

Library of Congress Cataloging-in-Publication Data

Kafele, Baruti K.
  The principal 50 : critical leadership questions for inspiring schoolwide excellence / Baruti K. Kafele.
    pages cm
  Includes bibliographical references and index.
    ISBN 978-1-4166-2014-3 (pbk. : alk. paper) 1. School principals--United States. 2. Educational leadership--United States. 3. School management and organization--United States. I. Title. II. Title: Principal fifty.
  LB2831.92.K34 2015
  371.2'012--dc23
                                    2014049240

24 23 22 21 20 19 18 17 16 15   3 4 5 6 7 8 9 10 11 12

This book is dedicated to the man whose leadership inspired me the most: Frank Mickens, principal of Boys and Girls High School in the Bedford-Stuyvesant section of Brooklyn, New York. He took over the leadership of the 4,000-student school in 1986, when it was marred by violence, a high dropout rate, poor attendance, and low academic performance. Mr. Mickens completely turned the school around through his leadership—he inspired students to learn and teachers to teach. As he led his school to national prominence, I watched with awe and admiration. His fire inspired me to want to teach and, ultimately, to lead. His example became a framework for my future leadership.

Frank Mickens retired in 2004 and passed away in 2009. Before he left us, I had the opportunity to meet him at an education conference at which I was presenting. Before my presentation, I walked up to him and introduced myself. He said, "Baruti Kafele! I know you! I have followed your work for years! I'm so proud of you!" I had no idea that he knew who I was, much less that he had been following my work the way I had followed his. That was one of the brightest moments of my professional life.

Thank you, Mr. Frank Mickens, for all you have done for children, and for all you have done for me.

THE PRINCIPAL 50

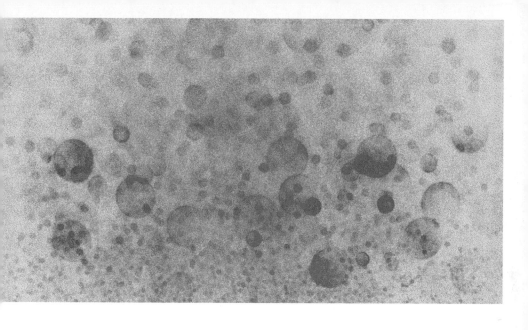

INTRODUCTION

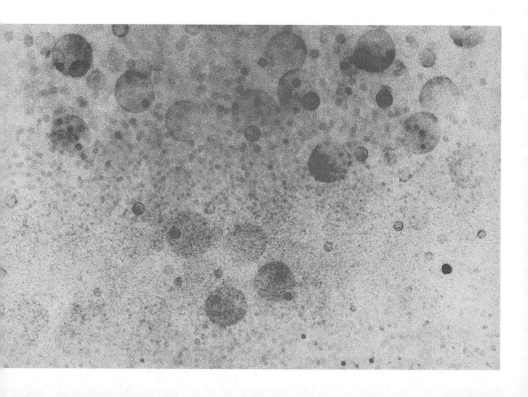

For 14 years of my life, I was completely devoted to the principalship. I worked in three challenging urban school districts in New Jersey, and despite the many struggles that our communities faced, I was fully committed to being the most effective school leader that I could be. To that end, I read everything I could get my hands on about school leadership, attended a multitude of conferences and professional development workshops, and observed and interacted with as many effective principals as I could. Why did I go to these lengths? Because I knew that *the more effective a school leader is, the higher his or her students will soar.*

I am now a full-time education consultant, and in this position I am sought out by acting and aspiring principals and assistant principals nationwide. Many of the acting school leaders who reach out to me maintain a limited scope of assignments and responsibilities, often because they work in schools with cultural challenges that relegate them to being school disciplinarians. I believe very strongly that a truly effective school leader must have maximum exposure to all aspects of school leadership rather than a narrow focus on meting out consequences to students.

This book is intended for all the principals out there who are looking for thoughtful answers to the myriad questions that accompany the challenges of school leadership at all grade levels and in all environments. The questions in this book are all offshoots of one essential, overarching query: *How can I inspire excellence from my entire school community?* This is ultimately the question that I want you, the reader, to keep in the back of your mind at all times. As you read this book, always bear in mind this fundamental truth: *The more inspired your entire school community becomes, the greater the chances that your students will achieve excellence.*

If you are an aspiring school leader, I strongly suggest that you envision yourself already in the profession as you read this book. Whenever aspiring principals and assistant principals ask me questions related to the careers that they intend to pursue, my initial response is always the same: "From this day forward, I want you to think as though you were already in the job. I want you to place yourself in the position and think and behave accordingly." Successful school leaders envision success as they prepare to achieve it.

If you are already working as a school leader, I want you to ask yourself whether or not the strategies that I suggest are a part of your current practice—and if they are not, I'd like you to consider how you might incorporate them. (The very last pages of this book are intentionally left blank for you to use as a space for reflection.)

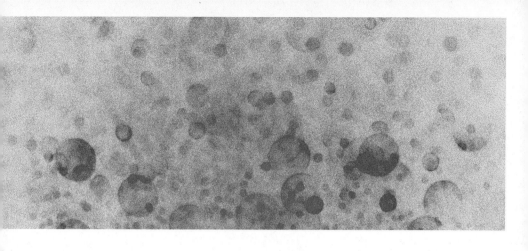

CHAPTER

1

The Attitude of the Leader

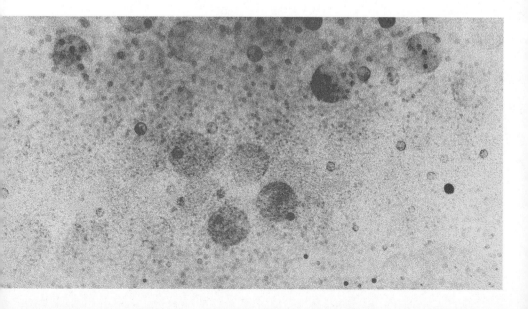

Q: Do I lead with a definite purpose that drives everything I say and do?

➤ Why do I lead?
➤ Why do I *want* to lead?

For your leadership to be successful, you must ask yourself these two questions daily. The answers to the questions represent your *purpose for leading*, which is certain to drive your approach to inspiring excellence in your school. Your purpose serves as a constant reminder to you of who you are—of what you are about—as a schoolwide leader.

I'm fond of the saying, "A person without a purpose is like a word without a definition—meaningless." You can't achieve maximum results without defining why you do this work in the first place. Why do you get up in the morning and come to school only to face the countless difficult challenges that crop up every day?

➤ Your purpose is *who you are as the leader of the school.*
➤ Your purpose is *the foundation upon which your passion is built.*
➤ Your purpose is *you.*

When I worked as a principal, I defined my purpose as follows: *To motivate, educate, and empower my students daily.* This was why I woke up in the morning—this was why I did the work that I did. My purpose drove me—it pushed me and pulled me. To my knowledge, I never deviated from my defined purpose. Additionally, I ensured that my leadership style reflected my purpose, making it evident to the entire school community. In order for me to inspire excellence in my school, I needed to motivate, educate, and empower students daily.

After you have defined your purpose for leading, you must further answer the following questions:

- Will I *walk* in my purpose?
- Will I *lead* in my purpose?
- Will my purpose *be evident* to the entire school community?

When you can answer a full-throated "Yes!" to those questions, you will be on your way to inspiring profound excellence in your school.

Q: Do I aim to be intentional about what I do as a leader?

- Random
- Reactive
- Responsive
- Haphazard

These four words spring immediately to mind when I reflect back on my first year as a middle school principal. During my first year, I reacted to situations as they arose, which left me "putting out fires" all day, every day. As the leader of the school, I *had* to respond to crises as they occurred, but doing so took me away from fulfilling my purpose.

As I grew in the principalship, I came to the gradual realization that a random and haphazard approach to events was not compatible with effective leadership. I needed to "step up my game" in a big way—to think and act with *intentionality*. In fact, over time, "intentionality" became my byword. I learned that if we as a school community were going to meet all the pressures and demands that were thrust upon us, we had to be able to spend our days *acting on our intentions* rather than *reacting to situations*.

The same is true for you. With all the pressures you will endure throughout your career, you do not have the time to devote entire days to taking a random, haphazard, and reactive approach to leadership. Instead, you must

➤ *Define* your purpose,
➤ *Resolve to be intentional* about living your purpose, and
➤ *Live* your purpose.

Every morning, before you get started for the day, *envision yourself living your purpose* so you can see beforehand what you are going to accomplish. This foresight will help you to turn your intentions into reality—you can now be constantly and consistently intentional both about student outcomes and about your students' daily school experiences. In high-performing schools, leadership focuses on creating memorable buildingwide experiences—the type that help mold students into successful adults. The key is to employ *intentionality* when creating these experiences for students.

Q: Do I treat my leadership as a mission rather than as a career?

➤ *Your leadership should be your mission.*

It's normal to think of what you do or plan to do for a living as a profession, a career, or a job. The problem with these labels is that they're limiting—they don't tell the complete story. I suggest that you look beyond these labels and consider what you do to be your *mission*.

I always say that if you want to stop a person on a job, all you have to do is put your hand up and say, "Stop!" By contrast, a person on a *mission* will refuse to stop. When you are on a mission, you have a completely different mind-set than you do when you are simply doing your job; you will not stop until your mission has been accomplished. I'll take an educator on a mission over one on a job on my team any day.

As you live out your purpose as a school leader, you are bound to encounter students who are dealing with a wide variety of life challenges—in some cases, challenges so great that they eclipse the importance of school for students. Among other negative ramifications, these challenges can prevent your students from understanding the correlation between working hard in school and achieving success later in life.

This is where you come in.

You have to think, *I don't care how great the challenges my students face are. They are with* me *right now, and I'm on a mission to see all of them achieve excellence!* When you as the school leader express this attitude in the things that you say and do, your students' chances for success increase exponentially. You are no longer defining what you do as a job, profession, or career—you are proclaiming it to be your mission, with the ultimate goal being the academic excellence of your students.

Q: Do I have a vision of what I expect my students to achieve?

➤ *Vision: the ability to see that which has been projected but has not yet been attained.*

To inspire excellence from your entire school community, you must possess and foster a *vision of excellence* that the entire school community shares.

I have said to countless educators over the years that earnestly envisioning success is more than half the battle. Unfortunately, I have met any number of educators who have told me that they simply cannot envision widespread success in their schools due to the challenges that their students have to endure in their homes and communities. I find this to be highly problematic. All school leaders, but particularly those in communities facing systemic challenges such as poverty, drugs, or violence, *must* inspire excellence by helping students and staff to envision it in action, and must also consistently reinforce their own expectations for the school. Ask yourself:

- ➤ What is my vision for my students?
- ➤ What will my students achieve?
- ➤ How high will my students soar?
- ➤ Can I envision where my students will wind up as a result of my leadership?
- ➤ Can I envision many of my students on the honor roll?
- ➤ Can I envision most of my students going on to college?

A word to the aspiring school leaders: The mission of the principalship doesn't begin once you become a principal—it begins once you have *made the decision* to become a principal. It is at this point that you must begin to develop a vision for how successful your students will be as a result of your leadership—a vision that must always remain at the forefront of your thinking. Be sure to encourage your school community to claim and take ownership of the vision: Schools that have a *collective vision of excellence* have a much greater chance of attaining success than those that don't.

Q: Do I see myself as the number-one determinant of the success or failure of my students?

When I ask this question in my professional development workshops with school leaders, it usually generates lively, passionate, and heated discussions. Some school leaders absolutely see themselves as uniquely responsible for their students' success. They believe strongly that once their students arrive at school, *those students belong to them*—the outside world and its influences no longer matter. Students succeed or fail according to the school leaders' overall performance. Excuses have no place in these school leaders' minds.

Then there are the other school leaders—the ones who find it impossible to take full responsibility for their students' education given all of the other factors in their lives. I remind these leaders that the success of their students boils down to the attitude behind their leadership: If students are going to soar, they require school leaders who will accept nothing less than excellence from them. This fact does not in any way diminish the significance of outside variables that may adversely impact student motivation or the roles of teachers and parents. But at the end of the day, school leadership matters. When the principal can maintain the attitude that his or her overall leadership determines the success or failure of the school, students will benefit greatly. As I like to say, "Show me a school with extraordinary teachers in every classroom but an ineffective principal and I'll show you an underperforming school."

You *must* see yourself as the number-one determinant of the success or failure of your students. How are you going to lead effectively if you lack the willingness to hold yourself accountable for your students' achievements? If you are living out your purpose at a low-performing school, how are you going to help it grow and improve if you are not willing to point your finger at yourself first? *Holding yourself accountable* and *refusing to fail* are key elements of successful school leadership.

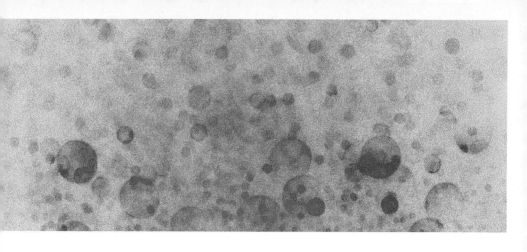

CHAPTER

2

School Brand

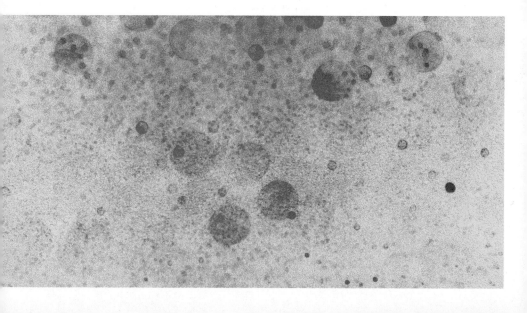

Q: Do I engage my staff in discussions about our school brand?

You must put maximum effort into establishing a common schoolwide identity—otherwise known as your school's "brand." Whenever I bring up the topic of school brands in workshops, I am met with blank stares. Branding is not a topic that school leaders typically discuss with their staff, yet it is essential to every school's success. Ask yourself:

➤ How does my school self-identify?
➤ Does my school's self-identification match the public's perception of it?

I cannot overstate the importance of discussing and shaping your school's brand with your staff. As a school leader, you can't afford to have staff with differing ideas of who you are as a school. Such disagreements inevitably lead to widespread inconsistencies for students that can affect the quality of their education. *Everyone in the school must speak the same language when describing the school's identity.*

At a minimum, your school's brand must reflect the school's

➤ Core beliefs,
➤ Values,
➤ Guiding principles,
➤ Purpose,
➤ Mission, and
➤ Vision.

Will your staff be able to synthesize and articulate the above elements as a school identity?

Think about your favorite restaurant, or car, or laundry detergent. Chances are good that you make these purchases because of your confidence in the *brand*.

Q: Do I ensure that my staff contributes to the development of our school's core beliefs, values, and guiding principles?

➤ What are your school's *core beliefs* regarding both the *practice of teaching* and the *process of learning*?

➤ What are your school's *values* regarding the students whose success you hold in your hands?

➤ What are your school's *guiding principles* regarding your staff's practice as educators?

When I pose the above three questions in workshops, the room often goes silent; educators don't tend to spend much time discussing these topics given the immediate pressures and demands that they must confront daily. I strongly believe that when we zero in on *who we are and what we believe,* we provide some missing context for our discussions of student achievement.

As a school leader, it is up to you to ensure that your staff contributes to the development of your school's core beliefs, values, and guiding principles.

Imagine a school with no core beliefs, values, or guiding principles that also happens to perform poorly. How can such a school improve when it has no compass to direct it?

Q: Do I ensure that my staff contributes to the development of my school's purpose, mission, and vision?

Every time I speak to a group of school administrators, I ask each of them about their school's *purpose*—that is, why the school exists and what rationale the staff has for showing up there to work every day. I don't want to hear generic responses—I want to hear the *specific purpose unique to the school*. I also ask these educators to recite their school mission and vision statements. Far too often, they tell me that they aren't sure—either they haven't memorized the purpose and mission and vision statements, or their schools don't even have them written down. I always tell them that I would not be able to lead a school that lacked purpose and mission and vision statements. I wouldn't know which way to turn, because these elements *define* the school and tell us the *direction* toward which it is oriented.

Ideally, your school's purpose and the mission and vision statements that are derived from it should drive everything you say and everything you do as the school leader. Having clear-cut statements of purpose, mission, and vision is crucial. If your school doesn't have these, drafting them should be a priority—and in doing so, it is vital to give all staff the opportunity to contribute to the three statements so that they have a sense of ownership and buy-in. Convene a meeting with your staff and begin the dialogue to truly cement your school's foundation. (If you are an aspiring school leader, you don't need to wait until you become one before considering the purpose, mission, and vision of your ideal workplace.)

Q: Do I have high standards and expectations for all of my students, and do I truly believe that they will reach them?

Most educators will tell you that they have *high standards and expectations* for all of their students—they go hand in glove with the profession. Unfortunately, these claims are quite often not true. It is absolutely vital that your standards and expectations be sky-high for all of your students, from the highest achievers to the most challenged learners. Your standards and expectations will make up part of your school's brand.

Key to maintaining high standards and expectations for all of your students is your overall belief in their ability to achieve. You can't realistically *expect* your students to achieve at the highest levels if you do not truly *believe* that they can do so. Undoubtedly, you will have students who come to school with a lack of belief in themselves due to factors outside of school. Despite these students' own doubts, you as the leader *must* believe that every single student who walks through the doors of your school can not only succeed but excel.

Q: Do I regularly reinforce the notion that my students will succeed specifically because they are enrolled in my school?

As leader of the school, maintaining and reinforcing academic expectations is one of your primary responsibilities. And your expectations for your students must be high *precisely because they are enrolled in your school*—you have made your school a special place for them, ensuring that it's an environment in which they will feel inspired to soar high.

In each of the schools at which I served as principal, I would tell my students that I expected them to succeed specifically because they were enrolled in my school. The last school at which I served as principal was Newark Tech. I would say to my students, "You *are* Newark Tech, young men and young women, and I expect you to perform and act accordingly." Consider crafting a similar statement to inspire your students to feel that they are in a unique environment specifically designed to ensure their academic success.

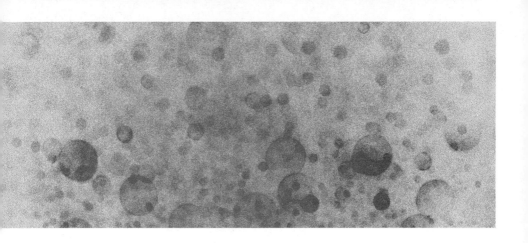

CHAPTER
3

Climate and Culture

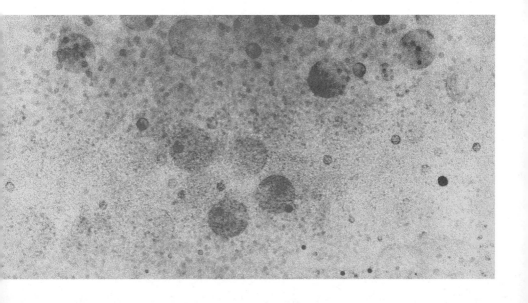

Q: Do I greet my students individually as they are arriving to school in the morning?

One might say that *school climate* reflects the "mood" of the school on any given day, whereas *school culture* reflects the "lifestyle" of the school—that is, the general way in which the school operates, day in and day out. One of the simplest yet most powerful things that you can do to ensure that both climate and culture are conducive to excellence in your school is greet students at the door each morning. Station yourself at the school's front entrance and greet every single student who walks in. Smile and maybe shake a few hands. Encourage your staff to do the same at the door of their classrooms. Telling students that you are happy to see them goes a long way. I am certain that some of your students won't have a more positive interaction all day.

I cannot tell you the number of schools I have visited where educators don't make it a point to greet their students in the morning—and I cannot overstate the importance of it. Greeting students at the door should be a nonnegotiable practice in every school. Doing so helps to accentuate the fact that your students are entering a warm and nurturing learning environment. When people ask me how I raised student test scores as principal, I always tell them that it started with the morning greeting.

Q: Do I set the tone for my school at the start of each day by delivering an informative, inspiring, and empowering morning message?

This is another area that too many principals overlook. It is imperative that you do all that you can to start your students' day off positively. Morning announcements are powerful tools for enriching the school climate and inspiring students to do their best. You can deliver your message in an assembly or via the public address system.

One effective strategy is to have a team of students deliver the first portion of the morning address. Students might use this time to

- ➤ Lead the school in a recitation of the school's motto,
- ➤ Go over standardized assessment objectives,
- ➤ Celebrate student birthdays, and
- ➤ Announce any good news relevant to the school.

When the students wrap up their portion of the announcement, it's your turn to bring it all home. Each and every morning, the goal of your message should be to *inform, inspire,* and *empower.* Your purpose at this time is to set the tone for the school day before teaching and learning begin. For these short few minutes, *you* are the teacher.

Q: Do I consistently strive to keep my students and teachers fired up about learning and teaching?

You must proactively strive to fire up everyone at your school so that they can approach their roles with enthusiasm. To this end, I highly recommend that principals deliver a "State of the School" address to the students and staff, preferably once every month.

I long ago came to the conclusion that a schoolwide address is a very powerful tool leaders can use to connect with the entire school community. I strongly encourage you to always hold the first such meeting of the year on the very first day of school, as a way of setting the tone for the months to come. When I held these meetings in my capacity as a principal, they typically lasted the length of a class period—plenty of time for me to discuss news related to student achievement, current school data, student behavior, and the overall climate and culture of the school. My primary objective for these meetings was to motivate my students and to inspire excellence from my entire school community. Your students will need constant

➤ Motivation,
➤ Guidance,
➤ Leadership, and
➤ Direction—all of which you must supply.

Schools in which the leader keeps staff and students informed, inspired, and feeling empowered have an advantage over those in which leaders serve only to flex their power and castigate.

➤ *Your students and staff must hear your voice—they must experience your leadership.*

Many teachers come in fired up at the start of the school year but find it hard to keep that fire burning as strongly over the course of the year. As the leader of your school, it is your responsibility to be cognizant of this reality and to address it by finding any excuse imaginable to keep teachers fired up as the year progresses. Infuse all your meetings and addresses with energy and praise; give your teachers high fives in the hall. I learned over the years that direct praise goes much further than gifts and luncheons. Like the rest of us, teachers want to know that they are appreciated and valued. Let them know!

Q: Do I ensure that the school environment is conducive to learning?

How much time and energy do you devote to what your school and classroom environments will look like on the first day of school? When I ask this question in workshops, the room often falls silent. When I worked as a principal, I would spend much of my summer break considering what I thought the hallways and classrooms should look and feel like on the first day of school. Frankly, it was something of an obsession—as it should be for you as well. Ask yourself:

➤ What will be on the hallway walls?

➤ What messages do I want the walls to convey?

➤ What stories do I want the walls to tell?

For my part, I've always wanted the walls of my school to *inform, inspire,* and *empower.* To this end, I made it a point to affix positive images and quotes on every wall in the building from historical figures who reflected the student body (in the case of Sojourner Truth Middle School in East Orange, New Jersey, this meant primarily African American historical figures). I also had material on the walls that reflected school pride and expectations. As the year progressed, we added material to the walls that reflected our students' achievements, including photographs, awards, and work samples. The intent was to create a warm, positive, and engaging learning environment for all students.

As you prepare for your first day, be sure that, at a minimum,

➤ All walls and stairwells are adequately painted,

➤ Halls and stairwells are immaculate, and

➤ Floors are shiny and waxed.

The walls of your school should also include the following materials:

➤ The school motto, mission, and vision;

➤ Motivational quotes and affirmations;

➤ Images of accomplished historical figures reflective of your student body;

➤ Criteria for academic excellence;

➤ Expectations for hallway behavior; and

➤ Signs, posters, and banners advertising as many colleges and careers as possible.

Q: Do I ensure that every classroom in my school has an environment conducive to learning?

The classroom learning environment is obviously of paramount importance. It is your job as a school leader to ensure that, from day one, all classrooms are up to your standards and compliant with district regulations. You should make it a point to tour your school daily, paying attention both to the teaching and learning that's going on and to the general environment. Ideally, every classroom in your school is a vibrant, welcoming, and engaging place that announces to students, "Come in! This is the place to be—this is where learning occurs!"

Because at least some of the students in your school are bound to face difficult challenges outside of school, learning environments should be designed to offset these challenges as best they can. Ensure that the following standards are met in all of your classrooms:

➤ Walls are painted,
➤ Floors are clean,
➤ Desks are neatly arranged, and
➤ Wall decorations meet the minimal requirements for the school environment (see p. 25).

In addition, I believe it is vital for all classrooms to have the primary objective of the lesson being currently taught posted in an easily visible spot. In fact, teachers should explicitly state this objective and have at least one student repeat it back on a daily basis. After all, how can we expect students to truly grasp lessons if they do not know the intended outcomes?

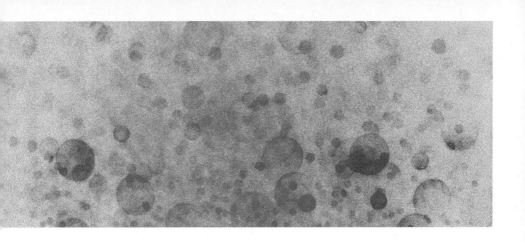

CHAPTER

4

Building Collegial
Relationships

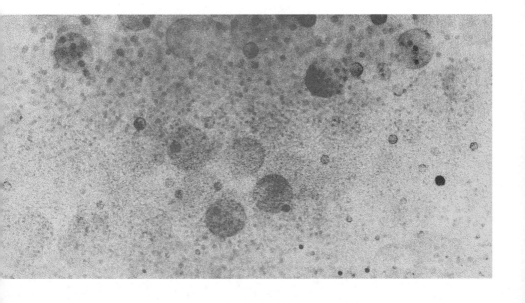

Q: Do I maintain a collegial relationship with my staff that supports instructional improvement?

The relationship between administrators and teachers at your school should never reflect an adversarial, me-against-them dynamic. When administrators and teachers work together, student achievement is bound to increase. Because administrators and teachers have the same primary goal—facilitating high student performance—collaboration should be a natural fit.

It is your responsibility as a school leader to ensure that teaching and learning are occurring at optimal levels in every classroom. To do this, you will naturally need your staff to trust you (and vice versa). For this to happen, you must first be able to convince teachers that you can actually help them to become better at what they do. If teachers do not trust you or feel that you have the professional expertise to make them more effective in the classroom, it will be difficult to establish a truly collegial bond. You must make every conscious and deliberate effort to establish yourself as the primary instructional leader of your school.

Q: Do I ensure that novice teachers are paired with competent veteran teachers?

Whether they're new to the profession or new to the building, new teachers at your school must be put in the best possible position to succeed. You want every new teacher to perform well enough to return the following year. Your relationship with each teacher is crucial: As busy as you undoubtedly are, you must still provide support by observing, mentoring, and offering valuable feedback to your new teachers.

Of course, you are not the only one responsible for ensuring that your new teachers are successful. As close to the first day of school as possible, team your new teachers up with competent veteran teachers who can serve as mentors and help them to grow.

Q: Do I encourage my veteran teachers to observe new teachers at work (and vice versa)?

Classroom observations should be an integral component of your school. Be sure to pair the most experienced teachers in the building with less experienced colleagues so that they can observe one another in action and provide one another with feedback. You must be extremely careful when pairing up teachers for this purpose, ensuring that there is a solid level of mutual trust between them. The novice teacher must sense that the veteran teacher truly wants to see him or her succeed; if not, the pairing will be counterproductive.

Though discussions among teachers about the specific areas of instruction that they will be observing should always remain confidential, as the school leader, you should have some input as well. Your role in the school is multifaceted and requires you to be surrounded by an excellent team. You must do everything you can to ensure that all the teachers in your building are effective—particularly the new hires. It's too much to expect them to do an excellent job at the very outset without the necessary mentoring. Instead, *put them in a position to win.*

Q: Do I participate in staff-team meetings and provide input and leadership when warranted?

Teachers in high-achieving schools are collaborative. They plan together, strategize together, and realize the value—the human capital—in one another. Effective teachers understand synergy and leverage it to enhance their practice, often through staff-team meetings. As the school leader, your participation and input in staff-team meetings (professional learning communities, grade-level meetings, subject-area meetings, and so on) are essential. Before you can participate, however, you must ensure that these meetings are occurring in the first place. Your guidance and direction are necessary to ensure that staff are engaged in meaningful discussions about student achievement. By participating in meetings, you demonstrate your commitment to your staff and to the overall growth of your school.

Q: Do I demonstrate my appreciation of and respect toward staff?

Your appreciation of and respect toward staff must always be more than evident. How can a leader even imagine moving a school forward without first demonstrating genuine gratitude for all that teachers do? Ruling schools with an iron fist only ever works in the movies. In real life, challenges both from without and from within the school often lead to tensions that can best be assuaged by truly respectful leadership on your part. If you have staff members in your school who tend to undermine your authority, your job is to win them over. *You must be able to establish a rapport with all your teachers* and not allow grudges or tension to affect student learning.

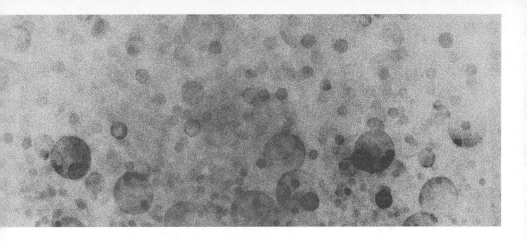

CHAPTER
5

Instructional
Leadership

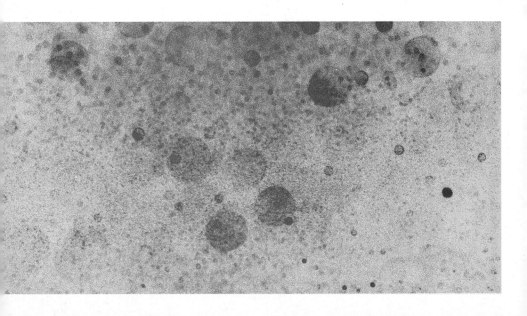

Q: Do I have a personal philosophy about how children learn based upon my own research and experiences?

As a leader at your school, you must be guided by a set of beliefs about student learning rooted in sound research as well as genuine personal experience. Your answer to this reflection question will surely evolve as you grow in your mission, but you must continuously give it serious thought—and beyond that, *take action*. Ask yourself:

➤ When you walk into that classroom, who are you?
➤ When you sit down with that teacher in that pre- or post-observation conference, who are you?
➤ When you are leading that staff meeting, who are you?
➤ When you are writing that weekly staff bulletin, who are you?

You are more than federal, state, and district mandates. The conclusions you've reached through study and experience shape your instructional leadership.

If you go into a classroom to observe instruction and learning but have no underlying philosophy, beliefs, ideas, or opinions about how what you are observing translates into learning, you are not in a position to make a teacher better at what he or she does, because essentially, you do not know. You know the mandates, policies, and guidelines, but in terms of what you yourself know and believe, you are at a disadvantage.

Q: Do I understand that my main priorities as a school leader are student achievement and the continued improvement of instruction?

Student achievement and *improvement of instruction* should be absolutely central to your mission as school leader. It is extremely easy to get distracted by the normal challenges of everyday life, but it would be a grave mistake to become consumed by reacting to them at the expense of these two crucial priorities.

I remember facing overwhelming challenges as a school leader in an urban environment rife with poverty and violence. Of course, the issues that cropped up in school were often of such magnitude and immediate concern that they deserved my full attention; the challenge for me was to address these concerns while still giving maximum attention to student achievement and improvement of instruction. These two goals require a school leader to spend a lot of time in classrooms, observing instruction—and, hopefully, student achievement—in action. To have the time for this, the school leader must *reprioritize* and *rethink* the way responsibilities are allocated within the building—by delegating the time-consuming work of extinguishing crises to trusted deputies among the staff, for example.

Any vaunted programs that you, as school leader, put in place to help raise student achievement *will be worthless without evidence.* If improvements aren't steady and significant, you must examine the efficacy of the program and consider pulling the plug on it. After all, *student achievement and improvement of instruction are your number-one priorities.*

Q: Do I spend most of my time every day observing classroom instruction?

You must spend as much time observing classroom instruction as you possibly can so that you can accurately assess the effectiveness of your teachers. Your presence in the classrooms serves as evidence that student achievement and improvement of instruction truly are your top priorities. Having said that, every school leader knows that making time to observe teachers in action can be a challenge. When I was a principal, I had a rule of thumb that I'd spend no less than a third of my time each day observing and offering feedback to teachers. Observation times varied from day to day, and my visits were, more often than not, informal.

You cannot lead from the main office. Reading e-mails and interacting with office staff have their place, but not during instructional time. During that time, your place is in the classroom, observing instruction.

Q: Do I ensure that the teachers at my school utilize a variety of instructional strategies in an effort to address the different learning styles, ability levels, and needs of my students in student-centered, culturally responsive learning environments?

You must ensure that your teachers' instructional practices are conducive to meeting the learning needs of all of your students. Ask yourself these two questions:

➤ What will you be looking for when you observe your teachers' instruction?

➤ Will you be in position to bring about desired results?

To properly assist your staff, you should be confident in the depth of your knowledge base regarding instructional theory and practice. Though there may be content-area supervisors at your school who share the responsibility of teacher supervision, the buck ultimately stops with you. *You* will be evaluated on the performance of your school, so the responsibility for it rests squarely on your shoulders. Never lose sight of that.

Q: Do I provide immediate feedback to my staff after observing their classroom instruction?

Providing feedback to your staff is absolutely critical for the cultivation of a high-achieving school. Teachers you have identified as needing the most improvement will require feedback the soonest—after all, the longer you wait to provide it to them, the likelier you both are to forget aspects of the lesson observed. Be sure, therefore, to arrange for post-observation conferences with them at the earliest possible juncture.

These days, of course, we don't have to sit around and wait for a scheduled meeting—it's perfectly reasonable to send a teacher immediate feedback electronically. In my years as a principal, I always made it a point to send teachers short e-mails immediately following classroom observation highlighting a positive takeaway from the lesson. My intent was to put teachers at ease so that they could focus on teaching and learning without being anxious about my feedback.

Feedback is what enables teachers to grow and improve. Without your feedback, poor teachers may assume that their instruction is satisfactory, and successful teachers may remain indefinitely anxious about their performance. Translate your focus on student achievement and improvement of instruction into immediate and meaningful feedback for staff.

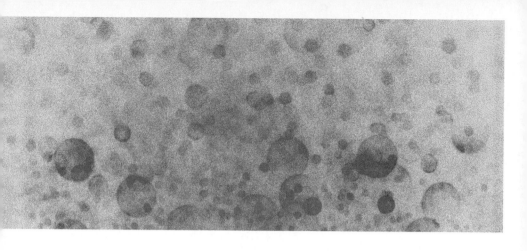

CHAPTER
6

Accountability and Responsibility

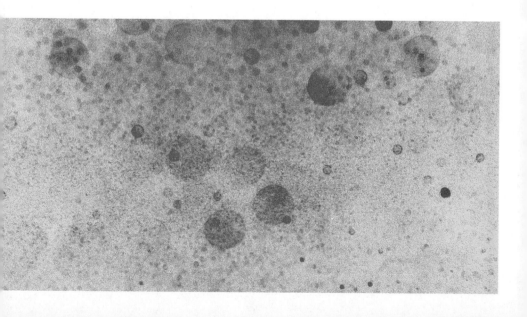

Q: Do I hold my teachers accountable for ensuring that all of my students strive to achieve academic excellence, including by meeting district, state, and federal benchmarks?

You must hold your entire school community accountable for the pursuit of excellence, and your standards must remain high for each and every one involved—but especially for teachers. Though you must always treat your teachers fairly when holding them accountable, your leadership must also be firmly established. *In order for your school to move forward successfully as one, you must be able to demonstrate your authority.*

Q: Do I refuse to accept failure, make excuses for failure, or allow failure to occur in my school?

You must make it known throughout the building that failure *is not an option* at your school. If you find that your school is replete with daily crises or that your students' lives are in constant chaos, will you still be ready and able to face the primary challenge of ensuring that your students receive adequate instruction? It's very easy to become distracted by the problems your school community faces or compelled to focus your energy on intervening in your students' personal lives. You simply cannot afford to let whatever issues are consuming your school to sideline you from a single-minded focus on improving student achievement. You must convince yourself that despite the challenges, your school will be successful largely because *you* are the leader.

Q: Do I accept responsibility and accountability for both my students' successes and failures?

As goes the leadership, so goes the school, so you absolutely must be willing to accept responsibility for both the successes and failures of your students. Of course, it's a lot easier to accept responsibility for the former than the latter, but shouldering blame when failures occur is the more important duty. It's easy and convenient to blame teachers or parents for poor student performance, but acknowledging your own role is what allows you to grow in your mission. You can't become a more effective instructional leader if you never acknowledge that improvement is possible.

Q: Do I model what I expect of my students?

Every school leader wears countless hats throughout the course of a day, let alone a year. One of those hats is that of role model for students. Always remember that your students are watching what you do and listening to what you say, even when it seems as though they aren't. And not only are they watching and listening, but they are learning as well—from your example. You must, therefore, pay close attention to everything you say and do. *You must model the right stuff.* (When I worked as a principal, I was well aware that many students looked up to me. I even saw some of them emulate the way I walked and spoke—a heavy-duty experience indeed!)

All eyes are on you, the school leader. You have a golden opportunity to serve as an example for your students to follow. And this status does not end when the dismissal bell rings: You are the school leader 24 hours a day, 7 days a week. Even outside of school, you must never lose sight of the fact that you are a role model. Be cognizant of the sort of places you frequent in the community, bearing in mind that your students or their families may also be at the same places. You should never put yourself in a compromising position that you have to apologize for later. This caution applies to social media, too: You must be painstakingly careful of what texts, photos, or videos you post online. As I like to say, we are all just one word, one thought, one photo, and one video away from disaster.

Q: Do I conduct daily self-reflections and self-assessments of my leadership?

When I was a young administrator, I had no idea just how important self-reflection and self-assessment would become to my practice. Rather than treat each workday as a part of one single yearlong continuum, I treated each one as a discrete entity. This perception fell away after I began to carve out time before and after work to "run the DVD" of my performance back to myself in my mind. This process allowed me to assess what worked and what didn't and to make the adjustments I needed going forward.

When engaging in self-reflection, ask yourself the following three essential questions:

➤ Who am I?
➤ What am I about?
➤ What is my most recent evidence?

I prefer to ask these questions directly of my reflection in a mirror. The first question establishes your identity, the second establishes your purpose, and the third establishes the evidence for the answers to the previous two.

It is essential to spend time reflecting on and assessing your relationship with the other administrators at your school, as it is crucial to your effectiveness as a school leader. The job of vice principals is to assist the principal—they are essentially extensions of the top leader. If you are a principal, you must regularly reflect upon how you treat and deploy your administrative team by asking yourself the following questions:

➤ Do I feel as though my relationship with other administrators is *healthy*?
➤ Is my team *loyal* to me?
➤ Is my team *committed* to me?
➤ Does my team *believe* in me?

➤ Do *I* believe in my team?
➤ Do I have *confidence* in my team?
➤ Will my team *go the extra mile* for me?
➤ Will my team *sacrifice* for me?
➤ Do the other administrators *fully understand* their roles?

If you are a vice principal, you must regularly reflect upon how you help to further the principal's vision for the school.

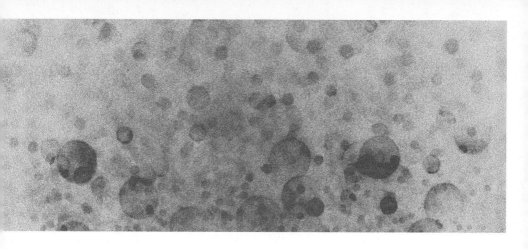

CHAPTER
7

Planning, Organization, and Time Management

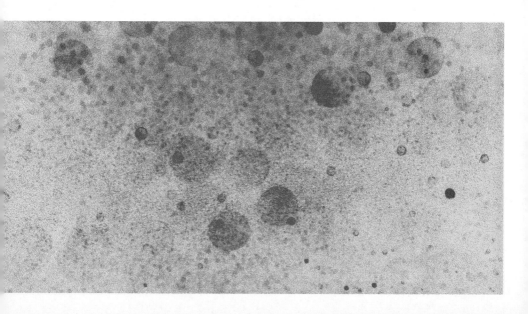

Q: Do I plan each day thoroughly while adhering to my own written plan of action for student success?

You must plan for excellence daily. As you know, teachers are regularly required to submit lesson plans detailing what they will teach over a specified period of time. These plans are important documents for you as an instructional leader. Not only do they let you know what your teachers will be teaching and what they expect students to learn, they also enable you to ensure that teachers' lessons are aligned to district expectations. But what about *your* weekly plans? Chances are good that you are not required to submit a weekly plan to a superior. Assuming that this is the case, what would motivate you to write out a plan of your daily or weekly activities? Leaders who plan are much more effective than those who don't because *they have determined in advance what they will accomplish and how.*

Think about what you want your day or week to look like and write down a plan of action that details how you will spend your time at work. Prioritize the actions that you intend to take. It's easy to react immediately to challenges that crop up when you arrive at work, but when you do so you run the risk of the day being consumed by your reactions to problems rather than unfolding according to your written plan. A plan allows you to anticipate at least some of the challenges that you're bound to face and decide in advance how you might address them.

Q: Do I ensure that I organize my day effectively?

Organization and planning go hand in glove: You can't have one without the other. It is impossible to achieve optimal success without being well organized. As an extremely busy school leader, you must have some sort of system in place that enables you to know exactly where everything you need is. Of course, some principals will leave the organizing in the hands of a secretary. Personally, I've always felt a need to be able to file and obtain important documents myself.

In addition to organizing your documents, you must organize your time. Your students abide by daily schedules, and you should, too. If today is Monday, you need to know where you will be and what will you be doing at 2:00 p.m. on Thursday. I have had fellow administrators ask me how I had time to spend three or more hours in classrooms daily. My answer is simple: I've always adhered to my plan and my schedule. I always made it a point to focus on instruction during school hours and to reserve time before and after school for other administrative work.

Q: Do I strive to empower my staff by engaging them in school-level planning and decision making?

You must give your staff opportunities to feel a sense of ownership for the operation of your school by asking them for input when engaging in school-level planning and decision making.

When I was a first-year principal, I was under the mistaken impression that all the power in the school lied within me and that my job was to supervise everyone else. I learned rather quickly that this approach did not bring out the best in anyone in the building. In my second year, I came to grips with the fact that just because I was the principal didn't mean I was the smartest person in the building. In fact, I had brilliant coworkers on staff who could handle more than their primary roles of teaching and learning. It was incumbent upon me, as the principal, to empower them.

You cannot afford to work in isolation. In order for your staff to *want* to assist you, you must focus on empowering them. One way to do this is by encouraging your staff to help develop or revise your school's mission and vision statements. Such statements mean something altogether different when they are developed with input from staff rather than imposed on staff from above.

Q: Do I use data to drive instructional decision making?

Identifying, interpreting, and utilizing data are tasks that require your full attention. When you think about it, everything that happens in your school is a data point. Data are being generated every second of the day.

Although your own creative ideas for improving your school are important, data are more so. We identify trends and patterns, explain behaviors, and tell the story of our schools using data. Especially salient types of data include those related to

- Tardiness,
- Attendance,
- Discipline, and
- Academic achievement.

Ask yourself:

- How will these data drive my overall decision making?
- How will they affect the way I lead my school?
- How will they influence my interactions with staff?

Q: Do I ensure that I am well versed in my district curriculum, state content standards, and state assessment specifications, and that I ensure they are taken into account during lesson-plan development?

As a school leader, you must be conversant in all aspects of instruction. In addition to knowing your district's curriculum, you must be aware of your state's content standards and assessment specifications. You should expect your teachers to teach to the standards and to develop tests according to state guidelines—and you should expect to see evidence that they do so in their lesson plans and in your classroom observations.

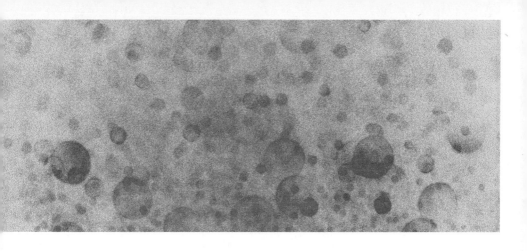

CHAPTER

8

Professional Development
for the Leader

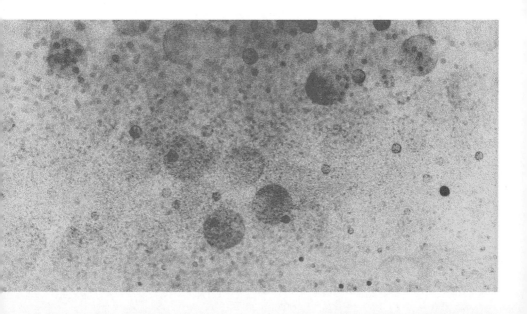

Q: Do I read professional development literature on the latest research in instructional leadership?

You need to read everything you can get your hands on in the area of school leadership. The most successful people around are those who "know that they don't know" and take steps to learn as much as they can about their work. Of particular importance to school leaders is developing an understanding of instructional leadership. It doesn't matter how strong you are in other areas—if you are weak and ineffective when it comes to instruction, you have little chance of improving scores in your school. Read all the books and journal articles devoted to instructional leadership that you can. Be sure to organize your days and weeks in a way that enables you to spend a decent amount of time on your own professional growth and development.

Q: Do I attend professional development conferences and seminars that address instructional leadership?

All school leaders must grow professionally. To do so in a way that really makes a difference, you must carve out time to attend professional conferences and seminars that address instructional leadership. Though many school leaders (myself included) prefer never to leave the school building during the day, it is imperative to take advantage of any professional development opportunities that come your way. Attending conferences also allows you to network with fellow educators from all over the world who have experiences similar to yours. The sense of solidarity that such networking engenders can be profound.

Q: Do I belong to any professional associations for educators?

Joining an association for educators is another way to advance your professional development. Such associations offer a plethora of information to assist you with your practice. Professional education associations typically host regional and national conferences that provide both training and networking opportunities. They also typically publish monthly journals and newsletters that can serve as great resources for you as you grow in your practice.

Q: Do I confer with colleagues and other educational leaders regarding my own professional growth and development as an instructional leader?

Successful school leadership requires ongoing professional development as well as consulting with peers in your school and district. There are sure to be some dynamite educators nearby who can help further your practice. No successful leader can operate in isolation, and there are many other school leaders in your community who are facing the same challenges as you and addressing them effectively. Forge relationships with your colleagues. Pick their brains. Learn from them. Shadow them when you can, and have them shadow you when they can. You don't have to wait for a conference or find time to read professional literature—there are leaders in your district who can assist you *now*.

Q: Do I and members of my staff visit schools with successful instructional programs?

When I was a high school principal, teams of educators would visit us regularly from different parts of the country. It was a joy to be able to provide them with answers to some of their challenges. I also had the opportunity to take teams to other schools. *You need to find ways to observe excellence in action at other schools.* Remember: You cannot afford to lead in isolation. You have *got* to network and forge relations with others—particularly those who have "already figured it out." Work with them. Collaborate with them. Most important: *Learn from them.*

Reach out to schools with similar demographics as yours either inside or outside your school district. Ask if you can bring a team over to spend a half- or full day observing classroom instruction and the overall operation of the school. We can become so inundated with our day-to-day work that we may not realize that there are more efficient ways of doing things.

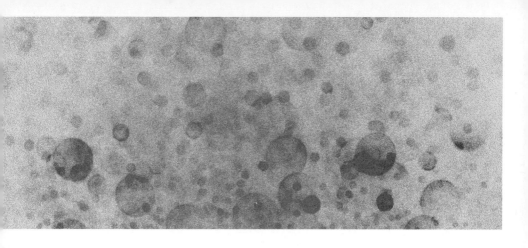

CHAPTER

9

Professional Development
for Staff

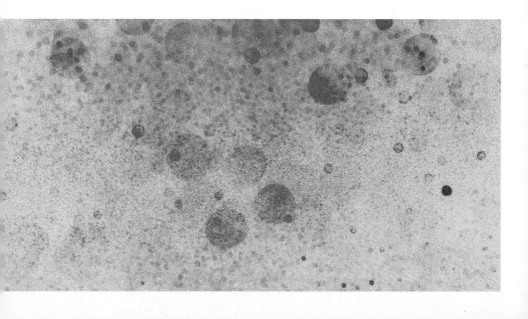

Q: Do I provide ongoing professional development for my staff?

Every successful school needs a well-informed staff. Your teachers must possess a plethora of strategies to effectively motivate, educate, and empower their students to strive for excellence. Are you providing your staff with the information they need to be at their best in the classroom? Consistent with your role as instructional leader is your role as *professional developer.* Part of your job as a school leader is to help teachers grow professionally, either by offering them suggestions directly or by providing them with professional development opportunities.

Q: Do I offer professional development opportunities during staff meetings?

When I was starting out as a principal, we would hold all-staff meetings twice a month. Because I was new in my position, I typically used this time to address any administrative issues among staff. As I grew in my principalship, I learned that I didn't need to spend so much time on administrative matters. Instead, I could devote meeting time to professional development led by myself, my administrative team, teacher leaders, or district supervisors. After all, administrative matters could easily be addressed via e-mail bulletin.

Your school has pressing needs. Pressure to raise achievement levels seems to come from all directions. You will
need all of the time that you can obtain to ensure that your
teachers are receiving the professional development that
they need for your students to excel.

Q: Do I engage all staff members during professional development staff meetings?

All staff must be engaged in professional growth. As the school
leader, it is incumbent upon you to ensure that everyone
at staff meetings is using the time to improve his or her
practice. This cannot be a time to grade papers or engage
in small talk.

Q: Do I regularly educate my staff by providing them with professional literature?

It is imperative that you keep your staff up-to-date regarding the latest instructional theories and research. There is
so much that your teachers need to know in order to be
effective. Though all of your teachers have most likely gone
through some sort of teacher preparation program, the
likelihood is that they've still got much to learn about edu-
cating students. A lot of what your teachers have learned
over the years in their formal training programs addresses

the *generic* child; now, your teachers are dealing with real, specific children. They must read everything they can on meeting the specific academic needs of the students in your school. For example, when I was a principal, the students at my school were overwhelmingly black and Latino. Regardless of the racial or ethnic composition of my staff, I had to ensure that they were equipped to successfully motivate, educate, and empower inner-city black and Latino students *in particular*. No matter the demographics of your school, you must ensure the same kind of focus on the unique set of academic needs of your student body.

Q: Do I engage my staff in book studies on pertinent topics?

Book studies or book clubs are yet another important professional development tool that can help keep your staff focused on what matters most in your school. Selecting books that address the specific academic needs of your students is a good way to get your staff thinking collectively about particular topics. This is a key component of your practice as an instructional leader and professional developer in your school.

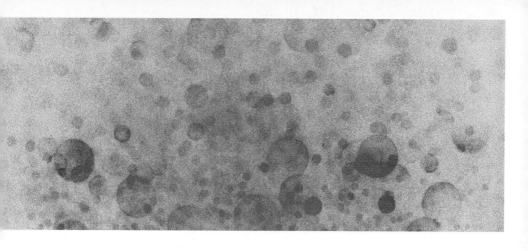

CHAPTER
10

Parental and Community Engagement

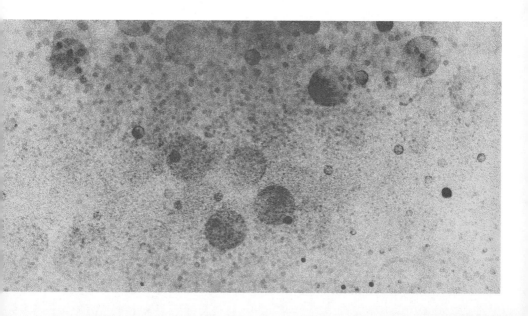

Q: Do I make parental and community engagement a priority in my practice as a school leader?

A satisfied and engaged parental and community support base can only help your school to soar higher. As I reflect back on my 14 years of school leadership, I realize there was never a time when parents and community did not play a significant role in the overall progress of the schools in which I worked. You must *intentionally engage* parents and community members—after all, the more hands on deck to motivate, educate, and empower students, the better.

When I worked as a principal, I launched two programs, one for young men and one for young women, designed to help students transition smoothly into adulthood. Both programs were quite comprehensive and involved all of our students, but succeeded mainly due to parental and community engagement. Without the crucial support of students' families and neighbors, the programs wouldn't have worked nearly as well as they did.

Q: Do I ensure that parents and community members feel welcome whenever they visit my school?

It's important to keep in mind that for many urban parents, schools can have unpleasant connotations. I can relate: By the time I got to high school, I had lost all interest and faith in school. Outside of athletics, I have very few positive high school memories. When I became a parent, I had some anxiety about visiting my children's schools due to the psychic baggage I still carried from my high school days. The only way for me to overcome that anxiety was for the staff at my children's schools to make me feel as welcome as possible. It is this insight that has made me go the extra mile to put parents at ease in the schools at which I've worked.

Ask yourself:

- ➤ How will parents be greeted at my school?
- ➤ How will they intentionally be made to feel?
- ➤ What kind of welcome signs will be on display?

Q: Do I include parents and community members in my school's programs and activities?

Engaging parents and community members in your school's programs and activities creates a powerful synergy with student achievement as the goal and can also significantly affect your school's overall morale. Of course, there are some programs for which parental or community involvement can be counterproductive. But for those that could benefit from the input, I encourage you strongly to include outside voices. The key is to bring them on board *with intentionality.*

Q: Do I aim to be accessible to parents and community members?

You must be accessible to everyone in your community, not only your students and staff members. In my days as a principal, I made it a point *not* to require appointments to see me. At our annual Back to School night, I informed parents that they could come see me at any time—but I also explained that I typically spent my days pursuing my goal of improved student achievement.

Make no mistake about it: As a school leader, *you want parents and the community on your side.* To that end, you must be intentional about winning them over. I learned over the years that I would need their support on any number of levels. Make parents and community members aware that you value them and their participation while also demonstrating that you respect their own time limitations.

Q: Do I aim to be receptive to input and ideas from parents and community members?

In addition to engaging parents and community members, you must be receptive to their ideas. Actively considering the input of outside voices enables those voices to feel a sense of belonging in your school.

Parents and community members cannot be adversaries of the school; *they must be allies*. When school staff can work as one with parents and the community, students benefit greatly.

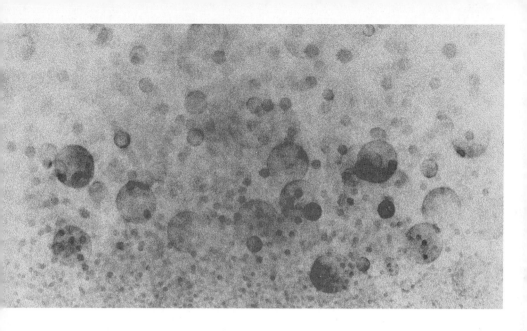

CONCLUSION

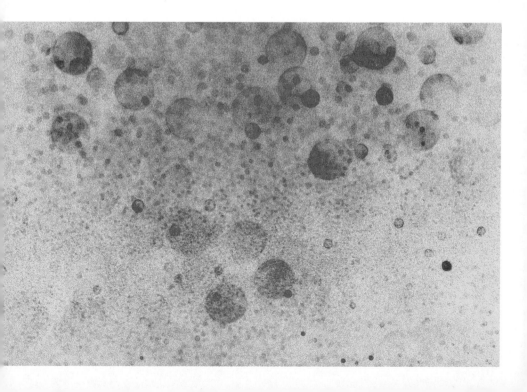

As I reflect upon the content of this book, I feel a sense of pride. Though it is the shortest of my seven books to date, it is also the one I cherish most. I have wanted to write this book for the past 15 years but didn't feel that I'd accumulated enough experience to write it until now.

Remember that I am a practitioner first and a scholar second—there is no theory in this book, only experience. I sincerely hope that this book will prove beneficial to you as you grow into your role as a school leader. Refer to it regularly throughout your mission for optimal effect.

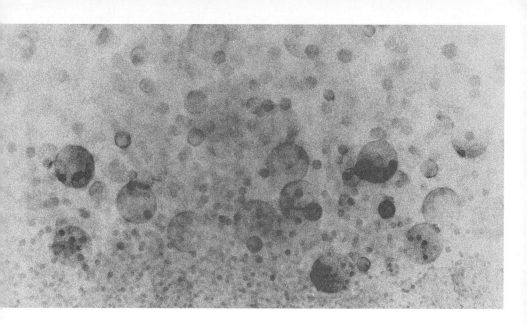

LIST OF 50 QUESTIONS

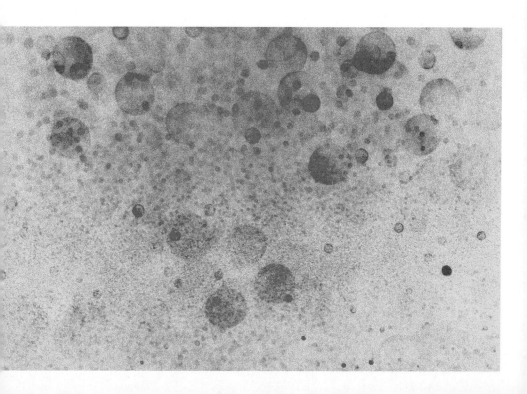

1. Do I lead with a definite purpose that drives everything I say and do?

2. Do I aim to be intentional about what I do as a leader?

3. Do I treat my leadership as a mission rather than as a career?

4. Do I have a vision of what I expect my students to achieve?

5. Do I see myself as the number-one determinant of the success or failure of my students?

6. Do I engage my staff in discussions about our school brand?

7. Do I ensure that my staff contributes to the development of our school's core beliefs, values, and guiding principles?

8. Do I ensure that my staff contributes to the development of my school's purpose, mission, and vision?

9. Do I have high standards and expectations for all of my students, and do I truly believe that they will reach them?

10. Do I regularly reinforce the notion that my students will succeed specifically because they are enrolled in my school?

11. Do I greet my students individually as they are arriving to school in the morning?

12. Do I set the tone for my school at the start of each day by delivering an informative, inspiring, and empowering morning message?

13. Do I consistently strive to keep my students and teachers fired up about learning and teaching?

14. Do I ensure that the school environment is conducive to learning?

15. Do I ensure that every classroom in my school has an environment conducive to learning?

16. Do I maintain a collegial relationship with my staff that supports instructional improvement?

17. Do I ensure that novice teachers are paired with competent veteran teachers?

18. Do I encourage my veteran teachers to observe new teachers at work (and vice versa)?

19. Do I participate in staff-team meetings and provide input and leadership when warranted?

20. Do I demonstrate my appreciation of and respect toward staff?

21. Do I have a personal philosophy about how children learn based upon my own research and experiences?

22. Do I understand that my main priorities as a school leader are student achievement and the continued improvement of instruction?

23. Do I spend most of my time every day observing classroom instruction?

24. Do I ensure that the teachers at my school utilize a variety of instructional strategies in an effort to address the different learning styles, ability levels, and needs of my students in student-centered, culturally responsive learning environments?

25. Do I provide immediate feedback to my staff after observing their classroom instruction?

26. Do I hold my teachers accountable for ensuring that all of my students strive to achieve academic excellence, including by meeting district, state, and federal benchmarks?

27. Do I refuse to accept failure, make excuses for failure, or allow failure to occur in my school?

28. Do I accept responsibility and accountability for both my students' successes and failures?

29. Do I model what I expect of my students?

30. Do I conduct daily self-reflections and self-assessments of my leadership?

31. Do I plan each day thoroughly while adhering to my own written plan of action for student success?

32. Do I ensure that I organize my day effectively?

33. Do I strive to empower my staff by engaging them in school-level planning and decision making?

34. Do I use data to drive instructional decision making?

35. Do I ensure that I am well versed in my district curriculum, state content standards, and state assessment specifications, and that I ensure they are taken into account during lesson-plan development?

36. Do I read professional development literature on the latest research in instructional leadership?

37. Do I attend professional development conferences and seminars that address instructional leadership?

38. Do I belong to any professional associations for educators?

39. Do I confer with colleagues and other educational leaders regarding my own professional growth and development as an instructional leader?

40. Do I and members of my staff visit schools with successful instructional programs?

41. Do I provide ongoing professional development for my staff?

42. Do I offer professional development opportunities during staff meetings?

43. Do I engage all staff members during professional development staff meetings?

44. Do I regularly educate my staff by providing them with professional literature?

45. Do I engage my staff in book studies on pertinent topics?

46. Do I make parental and community engagement a priority in my practice as a school leader?

47. Do I ensure that parents and community members feel welcome whenever they visit my school?

48. Do I include parents and community members in my school's programs and activities?

49. Do I aim to be accessible to parents and community members?

50. Do I aim to be receptive to input and ideas from parents and community members?

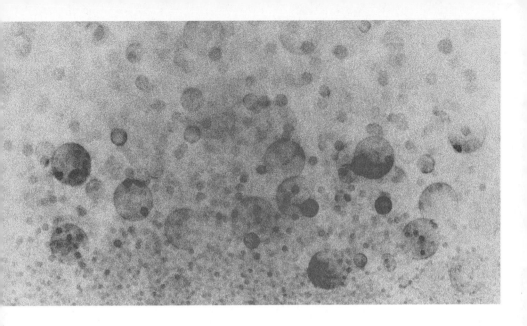

BIBLIOGRAPHY

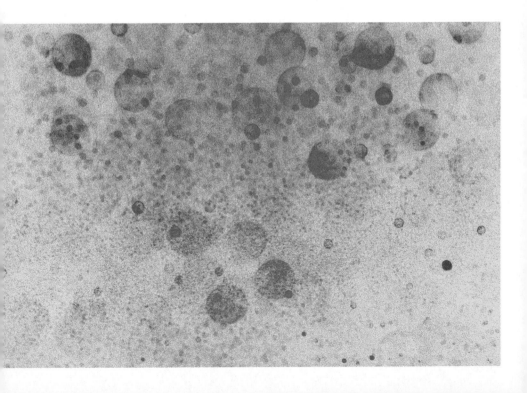

Breaux, A., & Whitaker, T. (2015). *Seven simple secrets: What the best teachers know and do.* New York: Routledge

Curwin, R. L. (2010). *Meeting students where they live: Motivation in urban schools.* Alexandria, VA: ASCD.

Kafele, B. (2004). *A handbook for teachers of African American children.* Jersey City, NJ: Baruti Publishing.

Kafele, B. (2009). *Motivating black males to achieve in school and in life.* Alexandria, VA: ASCD.

Kafele, B. (2013). *Closing the attitude gap: How to fire up your students to strive for success.* Alexandria, VA: ASCD.

Kruse, S. D., & Seashore-Louis, K. (2009). *Building strong school cultures: A guide to leading change.* Thousand Oaks, CA: Corwin Press.

Muhammad, A. (2009). *Transforming school culture: How to overcome staff division.* Bloomington, IN: Solution Tree.

Parrett, W. H., & Budge, K. M. (2012). *Turning high-poverty schools into high-performing schools.* Alexandria, VA: ASCD.

Rajagopal, K. (2011). *Create success: Unlocking the potential of urban students.* Alexandria, VA: ASCD.

Sterrett, W. (2011). *Insights into action: Successful school leaders share what works.* Alexandria, VA: ASCD.

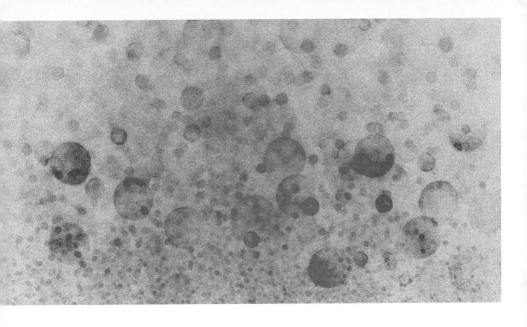

≫ ABOUT THE AUTHOR ≪

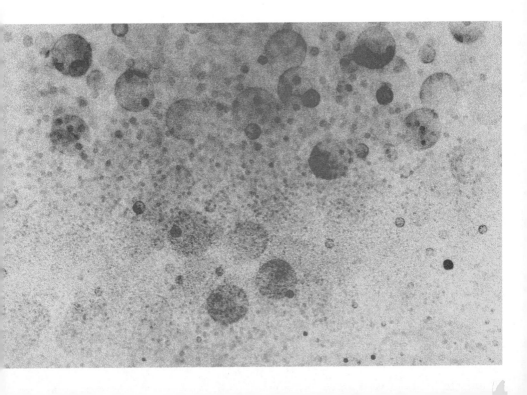

A highly regarded urban public school educator in New Jersey for over 20 years, Baruti K. Kafele has distinguished himself both as a classroom teacher and as a school principal. As an elementary school teacher in East Orange, New Jersey, he was selected as the East Orange School District and Essex County Public Schools Teacher of the Year. As a principal, he led the transformation of four different schools, including Newark Tech, which went from being a low-performing school in need of improvement to being recognized by *U.S. News and World Report* as one of the best high schools in the United States.

Currently, Kafele is one of the most sought-after speakers on the topic of transforming the attitudes of at-risk student populations in North America. He is the author of six books on this topic, including two ASCD best-sellers, *Closing the Attitude Gap* and *Motivating Black Males to Achieve in School and in Life.* He is also the recipient of over 100 educational, professional, and community awards, including the National Alliance of Black School Educators Hall of Fame Award, the Milken National Educator Award, and the New Jersey Education Association Award for Excellence. Kafele can be reached via his website, www.principalkafele.com.

A Space for Reflection

A Space for Reflection

A Space for Reflection

Related ASCD Resources: School Leadership

At the time of publication, the following ASCD resources were available (ASCD stock numbers appear in parentheses). For up-to-date information about ASCD resources, go to www.ascd.org.

Networks
Visit the ASCD Web site (www.ascd.org) and search for "networks" for information about professional educators who have formed groups around topics like "School Leadership." Look in the "Network Directory" for current facilitators' addresses and phone numbers.

ASCD EDge Group
Exchange ideas and connect with other educators interested in school culture on the social networking site ASCD EDge™ at http://ascdedge. ascd.org/

Print Products
Aim High, Achieve More: How to Transform Urban Schools Through Fearless Leadership Yvette Jackson and Veronica McDermott (#112015)

The Art of School Leadership Thomas R. Hoerr (#105037)

Creating Dynamic Schools Through Mentoring, Coaching, and Collaboration Judy F. Carr, Nancy Herman, and Douglas E. Harris (#103021)

Finding Your Leadership Style: A Guide for Educators Jeffrey Glanz (#102115)

How to Create a Culture of Achievement in Your School and Classroom Douglas Fisher, Nancy Frey, and Ian Pumpian (#111014)

The Whole Child Initiative helps schools and communities create learning environments that allow students to be healthy, safe, engaged, supported, and challenged. To learn more about other books and resources that relate to the whole child, visit www.wholechildeducation.org.

For more information: send e-mail to member@ascd.org; call 1-800-933-2723 or 703-578-9600, press 2; send a fax to 703-575-5400; or write to Information Services, ASCD, 1703 N. Beauregard St., Alexandria, VA 22311-1714 USA.